Pioneer Spirit
The
Westward
Expansion

SACAGAWEA

Rachel Lynette

PowerKiDS press.

New York

For Lucy

Published in 2014 by The Rosen Publishing Group, Inc.
29 East 21st Street, New York, NY 10010

First Edition

Editor: Jennifer Way
Book Design: Greg Tucker

Photo Credits: Cover, p. 20 Neftali/Shutterstock.com; p. 5 © Bettmann/Corbis/AP Images; p. 6 Tucker James/Shutterstock.com; p. 7 AndreAnita/Shutterstock.com; p. 9 © Interfoto/age fotostock; p. 10 Mark Newman/Lonely Planet Images/Getty Images; pp. 11, 16 © Adam Calabrese; p. 12 © AP Images; pp. 13, 19 MPI/Stringer/Archive Photos/Getty Images; p. 15 Superstock/Getty Images; p. 17 Manny Ceneta/Stringer/AFP/Getty Images; pp. 18, 21, 22 Marilyn Angel Wynn/Nativestock/Getty Images.

Library of Congress Cataloging-in-Publication Data

Lynette, Rachel.
  Sacagawea / by Rachel Lynette. — First edition.
    pages cm. — (Pioneer spirit: the westward expansion)
  Includes index.
  ISBN 978-1-4777-0782-1 (library binding) — ISBN 978-1-4777-0897-2 (pbk.) — ISBN 978-1-4777-0898-9 (6-pack)
  1. Sacagawea—Juvenile literature. 2. Shoshoni women—Biography—Juvenile literature. 3. Shoshoni Indians—Biography—Juvenile literature. 4. Lewis and Clark Expedition (1804-1806)—Juvenile literature. I. Title.
  F592.7.S12L96 2014
  978.004'9745740092—dc23
  [B]
                         2012046883

Manufactured in the United States of America

CPSIA Compliance Information: Batch #S13PK6: For Further Information contact Rosen Publishing, New York, New York at 1-800-237-9932

CONTENTS

An Amazing Young Woman

When explorers Meriwether Lewis and William Clark and their **Corps of Discovery** reached the land that is now North Dakota, they met a young Native American woman named Sacagawea. They decided to have Sacagawea join their group on their journey.

Although she was only around sixteen years old, Sacagawea proved to be a valuable member of the **expedition**. When Native Americans along the way saw that Lewis and Clark were traveling with a Native American woman, they knew that the expedition came in peace. Sacagawea also helped in many more ways. In fact, the expedition might have failed without her.

This painting shows Sacagawea with the Corps of Discovery as the leave Fort Mandan and head toward the Rocky Mountains.

At Home in the Mountains

Sacagawea's exact date of birth is not known. Historians think she was likely born between 1786 and 1788. She was born near the Rocky Mountains in what is today Idaho. When Sacagawea was born, Native Americans were the only people who lived in this area of North America.

Sacagawea spent her early life in what is now eastern Idaho, shown here.

The Shoshone hunted American buffalo. They hunted these animals for all of their parts, including their meat, hides, and horns.

Sacagawea was a member of the Shoshone Nation. Her father was a chief. During her childhood, Sacagawea learned how to gather berries, **tubers**, and other wild plants that were safe to eat. The Shoshone ate fish that they caught in rivers. They also hunted animals such as antelope and American buffalo.

Kidnapped!

When Sacagawea was about twelve years old, her people traveled across the Rocky Mountains to hunt buffalo near the Missouri River in what is now Montana. A group of **warriors** from the Hidatsa Nation kidnapped Sacagawea and several other girls. The Hidatsa were enemies of the Shoshone. The Hidatsa took Sacagawea 500 miles (805 km) east to live in their village in what is today North Dakota.

When Sacagawea was around fifteen years old, the Hidatsa sold her to a French-Canadian fur trader named Toussaint Charbonneau. Although he was much older than her, Charbonneau made Sacagawea his wife. Soon, she was pregnant with their first child.

This painting shows a Hidatsa village of earthen huts. When Sacagawea was kidnapped by the Hidatsa, she was taken to a village that may have looked like this one.

Lewis and Clark

Sacagawea first met the explorers Meriwether Lewis and William Clark in October 1804, when the Corps of Discovery built Fort Mandan near the village where she was living. The expedition spent the winter at Fort Mandan. They planned to cross the Rocky Mountains on their way to the Pacific Ocean in the spring. Lewis and Clark hired Charbonneau as an interpreter. They also asked Sacagawea to join the expedition as an **interpreter**.

This photograph shows a rebuilt Fort Mandan, where the Corps of Discovery spent the winter of 1804 to 1805.

When Lewis and Clark hired Toussaint Charbonneau, they hoped that his Shoshone wife, Sacagawea, would help them as an interpreter when they met with other Shoshone people.

On February 11, 1805, Sacagawea gave birth to her son Jean-Baptiste at Fort Mandan. When the expedition left the fort two months later, Sacagawea carried her baby on her back.

An Important Rescue

Sacagawea was a useful member of the Corps of Discovery. She showed the group berries and plants that could be eaten. She made clothing and **moccasins**. When Lewis and Clark had to make decisions about which direction to go or where to set up camp, Sacagawea was allowed to vote.

One day, Sacagawea was riding in a boat that her husband, Charbonneau, was steering.

This is a diary that William Clark kept during the expedition. Lewis and Clark's journals were important because they used them to record their observations and the new plants and animals they had seen.

This painting shows Sacagawea acting as an interpreter for the Corps of Discovery. She also contributed to the expedition by sharing her knowledge of which plants and roots were good to eat.

He lost control of the boat and it began to fill with water. Important **journals**, medical equipment, and books started to float away. While Charbonneau panicked, Sacagawea scooped up the things that were floating away. She saved nearly everything!

Returning to the Shoshone

When they got close to the Rocky Mountains, Lewis and Clark knew they would have to find the Shoshone. The Shoshone had horses, and the Corps needed horses to cross the mountains.

There were many Shoshone people in the area, but the ones that Lewis and Clark met in August 1805 turned out to be Sacagawea's own family! Her brother Cameahwait was now the chief. Sacagawea was happy to see her people again.

Sacagawea helped Lewis and Clark trade with her brother for the horses they needed. She helped them find guides to lead them through the mountains. They probably would not have gotten the horses without her help.

This painting shows Lewis and Clark meeting with the Shoshone. Sacagawea reunited with her brother during this meeting.

After the Expedition

The Corps of Discovery reached the Pacific Ocean in November 1805. They built Fort Clatsop near what is today Astoria, Oregon, and spent the winter there. The next spring, the group traveled back to the Hidatsa village. Sacagawea and her family remained there while the rest of the Corps of Discovery continued on to Missouri. Charbonneau was paid for his work on the expedition in both land and money. Sacagawea received nothing.

Here is the entrance to Fort Clatsop. Sacagawea and the Corps of Discovery spent the winter of 1805 to 1806 here.

In 2001, President Bill Clinton gave Sacagawea official recognition from the United States for her contributions to the Lewis and Clark expedition. A member of the Shoshone Nation and a member of the Hidatsa Nation are accepting the honor on Sacagawea's behalf.

In 1809, Sacagawea and her family traveled to St. Louis. The family left Jean-Baptiste in the care of Clark, who sent him to **boarding school**. Sometime between 1810 and 1812, Sacagawea gave birth to a daughter named Lizette.

An Early Death

In 1812, Sacagawea died from an unknown illness at a trading post called Fort Manual, in South Dakota. She was about 25 years old. Some Native American legends claim that Sacagawea did not die in 1812. They believe she returned to her people and lived until 1884. However, history has shown that this is probably not true.

Sacagawea has a gravesite on the Wind River Indian Reservation, in Wyoming, shown here.

William Clark

After her death, William Clark adopted Jean-Baptiste and Lizette. Jean-Baptiste attended school until he was eighteen and then traveled to Europe. He later returned to the United States and lived and worked throughout the West. It is not known what happened to Lizette, but it is believed that she died in childhood.

Remembering Sacagawea

The only honor Sacagawea received in her lifetime was when Lewis and Clark named a river in Montana after her. Since then, several mountains and a lake have been named for her. In Washington State, there is a Sacagawea State Park. Her image and the story of her contributions to the Corps of Discovery can also be seen in **exhibits** and statues in national parks along the Lewis and Clark Trail.

This is the 29-cent stamp that was issued in 1994 to honor Sacagawea.

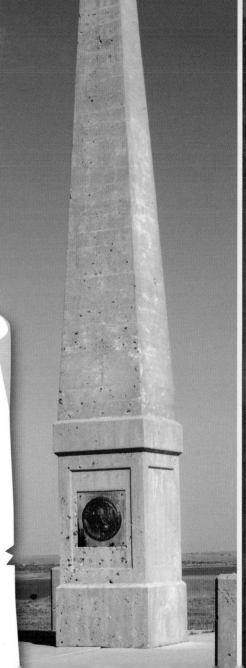

This monument to Sacagawea stands in Mobridge, South Dakota.

This trail marks the journey of the Corps of Discovery.

In 1994, a 29-cent stamp was made featuring Sacagawea. In the year 2000, Sacagawea's image appeared on the golden dollar coin.

An Important Woman

Lewis and Clark knew that without Sacagawea's help, the Corps of Discovery might not have succeeded. However, because she was both a woman and Native American, they did not pay her or give her credit for her work.

Lewis and Clark wrote in their journals about Sacagawea, though. Their words tell of a brave and **resourceful** young woman who played a major part in their expedition and helped bring about the **westward expansion** of the United States.

This statue of Sacagawea is in Cody, Wyoming.

GLOSSARY

boarding school (BOR-ding SKOOL) A school where students live during the school year.

Corps of Discovery (KOR UV dis-KUH-veh-ree) The name given to the expedition led by Meriwether Lewis and William Clark to explore the Louisiana Purchase territory.

exhibits (ig-ZIH-bitz) Public shows.

expedition (ek-spuh-DIH-shun) A trip for a special purpose.

interpreter (in-TER-prih-ter) Someone who helps people who speak different languages talk to each other.

journals (JER-nulz) Notebooks in which people write their thoughts.

moccasins (MAH-kuh-sinz) Native American shoes made of leather and often decorated with beads.

resourceful (rih-SORS-ful) Good at thinking of ways to do things.

tubers (TOO-berz) Short, fleshy stems of plants that generally grow underground.

warriors (WAR-yurz) People who fight in wars.

westward expansion (WES-twurd ik-SPANT-shun) The continued growth of the United States by adding land to the west and having

INDEX

WEBSITES

Due to the changing nature of Internet links, PowerKids Press has developed an online list of websites related to the subject of this book. This site is updated regularly. Please use this link to access the list: www.powerkidslinks.com/nswe/sacag/